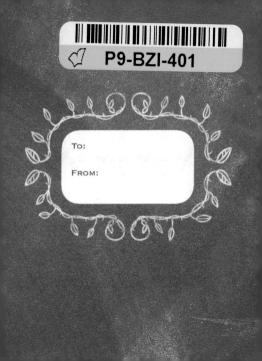

P9-BZI-401

To:

From:

FRIENDS
the family
WE CHOOSE

**WRITTEN AND COMPILED
BY JAX BERMAN**

PETER PAUPER PRESS, INC.
WHITE PLAINS, NEW YORK

To the friends who still put up
with my 4AM calls

Images copyright PinkPueblo, khandisha, Art'nLera, and
Peratek, used under license from Shutterstock.com

Designed by Margaret Rubiano

Copyright © 2015
Peter Pauper Press, Inc.
202 Mamaroneck Avenue
White Plains, NY 10601
All rights reserved
ISBN 978-1-4413-1831-2
Printed in China
28 27 26

Visit us at www.peterpauper.com

Fate chooses our relatives, we choose our friends.

JACQUES DELILLE

Let's face it. Life is full of ups and downs. But a good friend will be there even when times are tough. Our friends are our voluntary support group, the people we turn to when we need to share our problems, our thoughts, and our feelings. And we do the same for them. They are, in short, our own hand-picked family, ready to help each other out at a moment's notice. Just as good friends halve the burden, they also double the happiness.

Wise and warm-hearted like a good friend, this book is a tribute to soul siblings everywhere. Let it be a little reminder of just how important our closest friends are—the family we choose.

No friendship is an accident.

O. Henry

"We'll be
friends forever,
won't we, Pooh?"
asked Piglet.
"Even longer,"
Pooh answered.

A. A. Milne, *Winnie the Pooh*

How much *love* inside
a friend?
Depends *how much* you
give 'em.

Shel Silverstein

Friendship isn't a **big** thing. It's a million **little things.**

Author unknown

There is only one thing worse than *fighting with allies* and that is fighting *without them.*

Winston Churchill

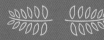

I have friends in overalls whose *friendship* I would not swap for the *favor of the kings* of the world.

Thomas A. Edison

What do we **live for,** if it is not to make life **less difficult** to each other?

George Eliot

My definition of a friend is *somebody* who adores you even though they *know* the *things* you're most ashamed of.

Jodie Foster

The most
I can do for
my friend is
simply to be
his friend.

Henry David Thoreau

When you're in jail, a **good friend** will be trying to bail you out. A **best friend** will be in the cell next to you saying, **"That was fun!"**

Author unknown

The essence of
true friendship is
to make allowances
for one another's
little lapses.

David Storey

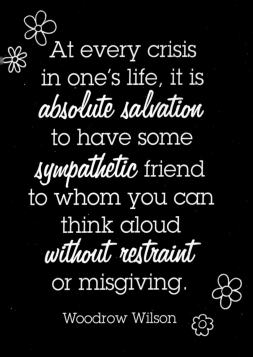

At every crisis in one's life, it is *absolute salvation* to have some *sympathetic* friend to whom you can think aloud *without restraint* or misgiving.

Woodrow Wilson

The holy passion of **friendship** is of so sweet and steady and loyal and **enduring** a nature that it will last through a whole **lifetime**, if not asked to lend money.

Mark Twain

It's the *friends*
you can call up
at 4 AM that
matter.

Marlene Dietrich

I would rather *walk with a friend* in the dark than *alone in the light.*

Helen Keller

Friendship ...
is not something
you **learn in school**.
But if you haven't
learned the meaning
of **friendship**, you
really haven't
learned **anything**.

Muhammad Ali

Friendship is always a **sweet** responsibility, never an **opportunity.**

Khalil Gibran

If you have two friends in your lifetime, you're lucky. If you have one *good friend*, you're more than *lucky*.

S. E. Hinton

Silences make *the real conversations* between friends. Not the saying but the *never needing* to say that counts.

Margaret Lee Runbeck

Hold a
true friend
with both
your **hands**.

Nigerian proverb

You can make more friends in two months by *becoming interested* in other people than you can in two years by *trying to get* other people interested in you.

Dale Carnegie

A true friend
is someone who
lets you have
total freedom to
be yourself.

Jim Morrison

True friends
are like
diamonds—
bright, beautiful,
valuable, and
always in style.

Nicole Richie

Each friend
represents a world
in us, a world
possibly not born
until they arrive,
and it is only by this
meeting that a new
world is **born**.

Anaïs Nin

Friend is somebody you give up *last cookie* for.

Cookie Monster, from *Sesame Street*

Being in a relationship, that's something you *choose*. Being friends, that's just something *you are*.

John Green

The friends with whom I sat on graduation day have been my friends for **life**. . . . We were bound by enormous affection, by our **shared experience** of a time that could never come again, and, of course, by the knowledge that we held certain **photographic evidence** that would be exceptionally valuable if any of us ran for **Prime Minister**.

J. K. Rowling

You just had to
decide who your friends
really were.

Terry Pratchett and Neil Gaiman,
Good Omens

A friend to *kill time* is a friend *sublime.*

Haruki Murakami

Mostly, you meet friends when traveling by **accident**, like by sitting next to them on a train, or in a restaurant, or in a **holding cell**.

Elizabeth Gilbert

We will *surely* get
to our *destination*
if we join hands.

Aung San Suu Kyi

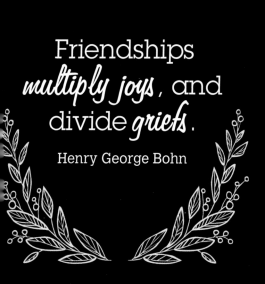

Friendships *multiply joys*, and divide *griefs*.

Henry George Bohn

In the **cookie** of life, friends are the **chocolate chips**.

Author unknown

We come from homes *far from perfect*, so you end up almost parent and sibling to your friends— your own *chosen family*. There's nothing like a really loyal, dependable, good friend. Nothing.

Jennifer Aniston

Some people
go to *priests*;
others to *poetry*;
I to my *friends*.

Virginia Woolf

I do not wish to treat *friendships daintily*, but with roughest courage. When they are real, they are *not glass threads* or frostwork, but the *solidest thing* we know.

Ralph Waldo Emerson

If you can find even **one person** you really like, you're lucky. And if that person can also stand you, you're **really lucky**.

Calvin, from Bill Watterson's
Calvin and Hobbes

It is a *nice reminder* that no matter how far you take it with your friends . . . you just really *need them*, because they're the ones who teach you the most about yourself.

Kate Hudson

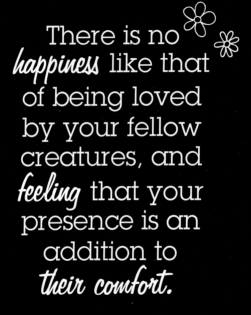

There is no *happiness* like that of being loved by your fellow creatures, and *feeling* that your presence is an addition to *their comfort.*

Charlotte Brontë

There are some things you can't share without ending up **liking** each other, and **knocking out** a twelve-foot mountain **troll** is one of them.

J. K. Rowling, *Harry Potter and the Sorcerer's Stone*

I suppose there is one friend in the life of each of us who seems not a *separate* person, however dear and *beloved*, but an expansion, an interpretation, of one's self, the very meaning of one's *soul*.

Edith Wharton

If we would build on a *sure foundation* in friendship, we *must love* our friends for their sakes rather than for our own.

Charlotte Brontë

The process of falling in love at **first sight** is as final as it is swift in such a case, but the growth of **true friendship** may be a lifelong affair.

Sarah Orne Jewett

Friends and good manners will carry you where money won't go.

Margaret Walker

A real friend is one who *walks in* when the rest of the world *walks out*.

Walter Winchell

The **better** part of one's life **consists** of his friendships.

Abraham Lincoln

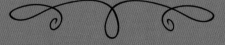

Do not bring people in your life who **weigh you down**. ... Good relationships feel good. They **feel right**. They're not painful. That's not just with somebody you want to marry, but it's with the friends that **you choose**.

Michelle Obama

Friendship
is magic.

Lauren Faust

But friendship is *precious*, not only in the shade, but in the *sunshine* of life.

Thomas Jefferson

Friends *cherish* each other's hopes. They are kind to each other's *dreams*.

Henry David Thoreau

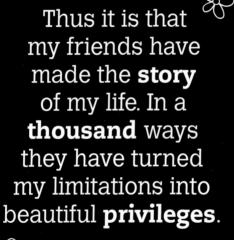

Thus it is that my friends have made the **story** of my life. In a **thousand** ways they have turned my limitations into beautiful **privileges**.

Helen Keller

Remember, George:
no man is a failure
who has *friends.*

Clarence, from
It's a Wonderful Life

But if the while *I think on* thee, dear friend, All losses are restored, and *sorrows end.*

William Shakespeare, *"Sonnet 30"*

The bird
a nest,
the spider
a web, man
friendship.

William Blake

Friendship has no *survival value;* rather it is one of those things which give *value* to survival.

C. S. Lewis

Friendship
is a
sheltering tree.

Samuel Taylor
Coleridge

Friendship is **love**, without his **wings**.

Lord Byron

Ah, how
good it *feels!*
The hand of an
old friend.

Henry Wadsworth Longfellow

And I think they knew. Not anything *specific* really. They just knew. And I think that's all you can *ever ask* from a friend.

Stephen Chbosky,
*The Perks of Being
a Wallflower*

Alone we
can do so little.
Together we
can do so much.

Helen Keller

It's such a
good feeling,
a very good feeling, the
feeling you know that
we're friends.

Fred Rogers

Love is only *chatter,*
Friends are all *that matter.*

Frank Gelett Burgess

The language of
Friendship is
not words, but
meanings. It is
an intelligence
above language.

Henry David Thoreau

"Stay" is a
charming word
in a friend's
vocabulary.

Amos Bronson Alcott

Fate chooses our *relatives*, we choose our *friends*.

Jacques Delille

Best friend,
my **well-spring**
in the
wilderness!

George Eliot

When friends
meet, hearts
warm.

Proverb

A *friend* is a person with whom I may be *sincere*. Before him, I may think *aloud*.

Ralph Waldo Emerson

Your friend is your needs **answered**. He is your field which you sow with love and reap with **thanksgiving**. And he is your board and your fireside. For you come to him with your hunger, and you seek him for **peace**.

Kahlil Gibran

What is a friend? A single soul dwelling in two bodies.

Aristotle

Some friendships
are made by
nature, some by
contract, some
by interest, and
some by *souls*.

Jeremy Taylor

There is **nothing**
I would not do for
those who are really
my friends. I have
no notion of loving
people **by halves**;
it is not my nature.

Jane Austen,
Northanger Abbey

The typical expression of *opening* Friendship would be something like, "What? You too? I thought I was the *only one*."

C. S. Lewis

Friendship is the only cement that will *ever hold* the world *together*.

Woodrow Wilson